EXAMINING
HURRICANES

BY SABRINA KIDD

CLARA
HOUSE
BOOKS

First published in 2015 by Clara House Books, an imprint of
The Oliver Press, Inc.

Clara House Books
5707 West 36th Street
Minneapolis, MN 55416
USA

Editors: Mirella Miller and Arnold Ringstad
Series Designer: Maggie Villaume

Picture Credits
Zacarias Pereira da Mata/Shutterstock Images, cover, 1; Shutterstock Images, 4, 30; Red Line
Editorial, 7; Shannon Ruvelas/Shutterstock Images, 8–9; Anton Oparin/Shutterstock Images,
11; NASA, 12; NASA/Corbis, 15; Thinkstock, 17; John Plumber/DK Images, 18; Library of
Congress, 20; NOAA, 23, 24–25, 34; FEMA, 27; Eric Gay/AP Images, 28; Glynnis Jones/
Shutterstock Images, 32; Zack Frank/Shutterstock Images, 36; David J. Phillip/AP Images,
38–39; Sayre Berman/Corbis, 41

Library of Congress Cataloging-in-Publication Data

Kidd, Sabrina, 1972-
  Examining hurricanes / by Sabrina Kidd.
     pages cm – (Examining disasters)
  Includes index.
  Audience: 7 to 8.
  ISBN 978-1-934545-64-5 (hardcover : alk. paper)
  1. Hurricanes–Juvenile literature. I. Title. II. Series: Examining disasters.
  QC944.2.K54 2015
  551.55'2–dc23

                              2014044473

Printed in the United States of America
CG1022015

www.oliverpress.com

CONTENTS

ONE

SUPERSTORM

Hurricanes are the world's largest, most destructive storms. Their swirling masses of wind and water can destroy cities, take lives, and leave thousands of people without homes. One of the worst hurricanes in recent history hit the East Coast of the United States in late October 2012. The media nicknamed it Superstorm Sandy.

Superstorm Sandy began to take shape on October 19, 2012, in the Atlantic Ocean. By October 22, Sandy had traveled west to the Caribbean Sea. Four days later, its wind speeds increased and Sandy became a tropical storm. Sandy turned north and was upgraded to a Category 1 hurricane, the weakest level, just before it hit Jamaica on October 24. Early in the morning of October 25, the

Homes along the East Coast of the United States were destroyed in Superstorm Sandy's path.

U.S. National Hurricane Center (NHC) officials upgraded Sandy to a Category 2 hurricane. Its winds whipped at 110 miles (177 km) per hour. Sandy's eye, the center of the storm, passed over Jamaica and Cuba. It ripped trees out of the ground, tore roofs off houses, and destroyed crops.

Sandy continued its destructive path through the Caribbean. In Haiti, many people were living in temporary shelters because a massive earthquake had struck the country in 2010, destroying many homes. Superstorm Sandy blew many of the shelters away, leaving 200,000 people with nowhere to live. It was the country's second weather-related disaster in two years.

But Sandy was not finished yet. By the time it reached the East

NAMING HURRICANES

The World Meteorological Organization (WMO) names hurricanes to avoid confusion when two or more form in the same part of the world. The names also make it easier to inform the public about a particular storm. The names come from an alphabetical list maintained by the WMO. Storms switch between male and female names. When a storm is so deadly or costly that its name seems inappropriate for future use, the name is removed from the list. Sandy was replaced by the name Sara on the list.

CATEGORY	WIND SPEED	ESTIMATED DAMAGE
1	74–95 miles (119–153 km) per hour	Dangerous winds; damage will occur
2	96–110 miles (154–177 km) per hour	Extremely dangerous winds; extensive damage will occur
3	111–129 miles (178–208 km) per hour	Devastating damage will occur
4	130–156 miles (209–251 km) per hour	Catastrophic damage will occur
5	157+ miles (252+ km) per hour	Catastrophic damage will occur

SAFFIR-SIMPSON HURRICANE SCALE
This scale gives a 1 to 5 rating based on a hurricane's sustained wind speed. A Category 3 or higher is considered a major hurricane.

Coast of the United States, the superstorm was 900 miles (1,450 km) wide—the distance between New York City and Atlanta, Georgia. Giant waves crushed the coast of

Wind and water destroyed the downtown boardwalk in New Jersey's historic Atlantic City, dragging the Jet Star roller coaster into the ocean.

New York and New Jersey. Waves as large as 14 feet (4 m) called storm surges flooded New York City's streets.

AFTERMATH OF SUPERSTORM SANDY

Sandy killed more than 200 people in the seven countries it struck, and caused approximately $65 billion in damage. The only hurricane to cause more damage to property was Hurricane Katrina in 2005. Approximately

SEISMIC ACTIVITY

The ocean waves caused by Superstorm Sandy were so powerful they caused seismic waves, the kind of waves involved in earthquakes. The waves caused vibrations detected by seismometers designed to detect such activity and warn about possible earthquakes. While earthquake waves happen in quick bursts, the vibrations from Sandy occurred gradually over time as the hurricane moved along the coast. Although the seismic activity was small, the seismometer data was used to supplement satellite and other weather data.

8.5 million people in the United States lost power due to Sandy. More than 20,000 flights were canceled along the East Coast, trains stopped running, and cars had trouble navigating roads that were flooded or blocked by debris. Sandy was one of the costliest disasters in U.S. history, both in terms of dollars and lives.

TWO

HURRICANE FORMATION

Hurricanes that form in the Atlantic Ocean, the Northeast Pacific Ocean, and the Gulf of Mexico affect the United States, Mexico, and the Caribbean islands. Hurricanes can also hit Asia, Australia, and Africa. These Pacific Ocean storms are called typhoons or cyclones but are the same type of storms as hurricanes. Meteorologists group hurricanes, typhoons, and cyclones under the term tropical cyclone.

Tropical cyclones form around low-pressure systems, which are areas where air pressure is lower than the pressure of the surrounding atmosphere. A low-pressure system develops when warm, moist air rises in the atmosphere.

Superstorm Sandy's storm system was large enough to be seen from space.

HURRICANE SIZE

Hurricanes average approximately 300 miles (480 km) across, but their size varies widely. Typhoon Tip hit Japan on October 12, 1979. It measured approximately 1,350 miles (2,170 km) across, making it the largest hurricane on record. Tropical Storm Marco was among the smallest. It was just 86 miles (138 km) wide when it struck Mexico on October 7, 2008.

As the warm air rises, it cools and condenses into tiny droplets of water. The droplets form into clouds which can produce thunderstorms.

Tropical cyclones are rotating systems of clouds and thunderstorms that are created over warm water. Occasionally, if several thunderstorms are near each other, they blend into one. Such a storm system might turn into a hurricane, or it might break apart. Certain conditions must be in place for the storm system to progress from a tropical depression to a tropical storm or, eventually, to a hurricane.

CHANGING STORMS

If a storm system continues to rotate for at least 24 hours without breaking apart, it is called a tropical disturbance. As its wind speeds increase, the storm begins to rotate. When its wind speeds range between 23 and 38 miles

Sep 6 2008

Hurricanes form more easily in warmer water, shown here in red, orange, and yellow.

(37 and 61 km) per hour, the system is called a tropical depression.

For a tropical cyclone to develop, a system must begin over water that is at least 80 degrees Fahrenheit (26°C).

The ocean water evaporates and creates warm, moisture-filled air. Next, light winds from different directions meet and force the warm air upward, leaving less at the surface. Cooler air rushes in to replace the warm air. This air warms and rises, too. Higher in the atmosphere, the humid air cools, creating more clouds and thunderstorms. Some of the cooler air is pushed over the storm and sinks back down to the ocean surface. It picks up warmth and moisture from the ocean and rises again. The cluster of

HOW SCIENCE WORKS
A SELF-FEEDING MACHINE

A hurricane draws its power from the energy provided by warm ocean water. At the center of a hurricane is a relatively calm area called the eye. Surrounding the eye is an area called the eyewall that contains the strongest winds and heaviest thunderstorms of the hurricane. It is formed as warm air rushes inward and turns upward into the storm. Finally, rainbands whirl around the entire structure like giant pinwheels. Each of these structures plays its own role in keeping the hurricane intact.

In the eye and around the rainbands, air from higher in the atmosphere sinks toward the ocean surface. Sinking air warms and dries, creating a mostly cloud-free, rain-free eye. Meanwhile, low pressure at the ocean surface pulls in air from the surrounding area. This warm, moist air swirls into the eyewall and rainbands. The warm air rises and cools, and its water vapor condenses into rain. This process releases large amounts of heat, and wind speeds increase, pulling more moisture into the storm.

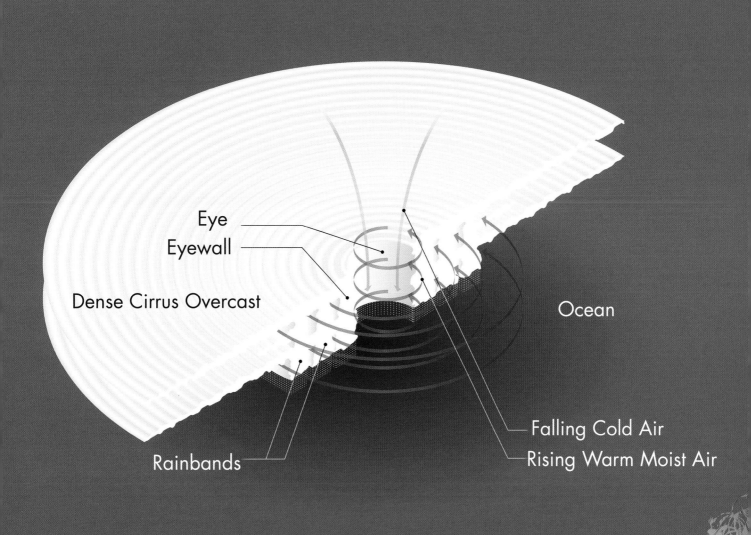

Eye

Eyewall

Dense Cirrus Overcast

Ocean

Falling Cold Air

Rising Warm Moist Air

Rainbands

The Coriolis effect gives a tropical cyclone its spinning motion.

storms grows bigger and stronger. It begins to spin around its low-pressure system.

Because Earth rotates, the rushing air curves, in what is known as the Coriolis effect. A storm north of the Equator spins in a counterclockwise direction. Storms south of the Equator spin in a clockwise direction.

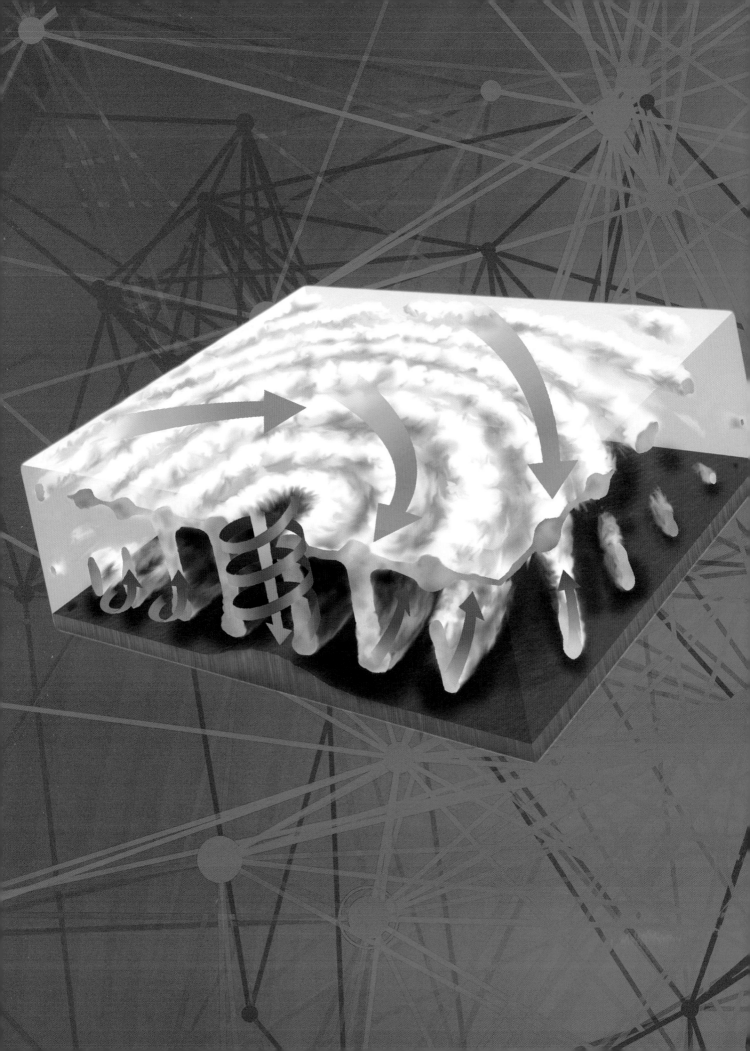

BECOMING A HURRICANE

A tropical depression becomes a tropical storm when its wind speeds range between 39 and 73 miles (63 and 117 km) per hour. At that point, the storm is considered serious enough to be given a name. Once winds reach a speed of 74 miles (119 km) per hour or higher, the storm becomes a hurricane.

As long as nothing breaks the cycle, the storm will continue to suck warmth out of the ocean and use it to grow bigger and stronger. Hurricanes begin to break apart when they move over land or reach areas of cooler water. Without warm water to fuel them, the storms soon lose strength.

HURRICANE SEASON

Hurricanes form during the warm months, because ocean water is the warmest then. Solar radiation, or energy from the sun, is strongest on December 22 in the Southern Hemisphere and on June 22 in the Northern Hemisphere. The tropical oceans fully heat up a few weeks after these dates. Most hurricanes form in the months of August and September.

THREE

TRACKING AND PREDICTING

In the early 1900s, hurricane tracking was much different. People living in hurricane-prone areas did not know when hurricanes were approaching. Meteorologists typically received information about storms at sea when ships came into port. Weather offices kept in touch with each other by telephone and telegraph. If telephone or telegraph lines broke down, so did communication. Meteorologists used tools such as barometers, anemometers, rain gauges, and thermometers to measure conditions as a hurricane approached land. However, these tools provided little advance warning of incoming storms. Hurricane death tolls were dramatically

Huge parts of Galveston, Texas, were completely ruined by the 1900 hurricane.

larger than today. For example, the hurricane that hit Galveston, Texas, on September 8, 1900, left one city in ruins.

Without modern weather forecasting tools to warn them, residents of Galveston were taken by surprise when the Great Galveston Hurricane destroyed their city. At least 6,000 of Galveston's approximately 40,000 people lost their lives. Thousands more from the surrounding area died as well. This terrible loss of life made the hurricane the deadliest ever to hit the United States.

TRACKING TOOLS

Today, meteorologists use a huge collection of tools to track hurricanes. Some of the most important tools are the Geostationary Operational Environmental Satellites (GOES). The GOES system tracks storms and helps meteorologists predict weather. This group of satellites circles Earth approximately 22,300 miles (35,900 km) above the surface. The satellites move at the same speed that Earth spins, meaning each satellite stays above a fixed point on Earth's surface. Then the satellites can

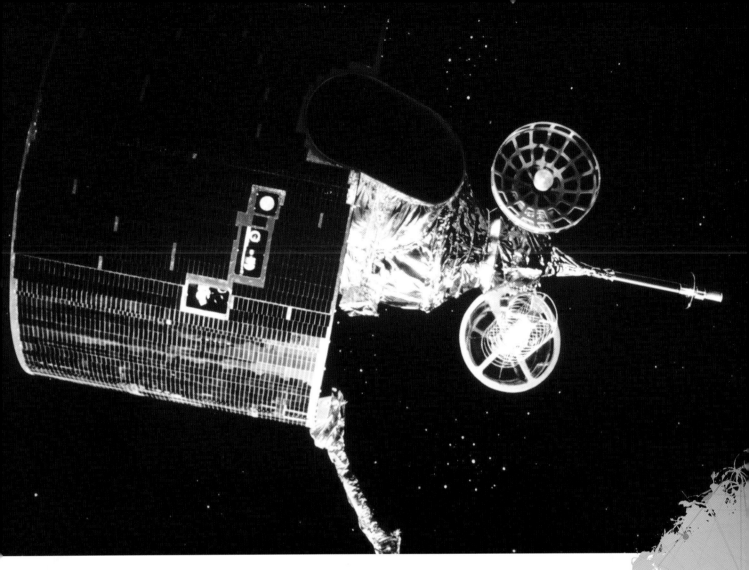

GOES are large and contain several scientific instruments.

monitor a particular area for any conditions that might trigger a hurricane.

Pilots called hurricane hunters fly special airplanes directly into the eyes of hurricanes. Once they get the plane into the proper position, the pilots drop an instrument called a dropsonde into the hurricane. The dropsonde measures a storm's wind speed, air pressure, and humidity. The instrument sends that information to meteorologists' computers.

Hurricane hunter planes fly at a height between 1,000 and 10,000 feet (305–3,050 m).

HELPING PEOPLE ON THE GROUND

Meteorologists on the ground interpret information. Then they provide information to public officials and local news stations. People living in places where a hurricane is headed can prepare for the storm. Many people nail wooden boards over their windows to protect the glass. They stock up on food, water, and medicine if they decide to stay in their homes. If the hurricane is predicted

to be severe, people sometimes choose to leave the area. Governments may even order an evacuation, requiring or recommending that people in a certain area leave, to keep people safe.

But evacuation orders are not always effective. When Hurricane Katrina struck New Orleans, Louisiana, in August 2005, tens of thousands of residents could not or would not leave the city. Some did not want to leave their homes and thought they could survive the storm.

The city had a series of levees, a system of man-made walls that protected residential areas from surges in lakes and other bodies of water. Several of these barriers broke under the force of the hurricane's wind, rain, and storm surge. The storm surged over the top of some levees, and others broke due to design faults, leaving parts of the city under more than 10 feet (3 m) of water. The residents stuck in the city did not have access to food, water, medicine, or any means of escape. Hurricane Katrina and the ensuing chaos killed 1,800 people across the South and devastated the city of New Orleans.

The U.S. Army Corps of Engineers (USACE) has been working on building new systems in New Orleans since Hurricane Katrina. These systems include new levees, floodwalls, and storm surge barriers.

THE FIRST FLIGHT INTO A HURRICANE

Hurricane hunting began on July 27, 1943. Col. Joseph Duckworth and Lt. Ralph O'Hair of the U.S. Army took an unplanned flight into a hurricane that hit the Texas coast. They braved the high winds, gathered information about the storm, and safely made it back to the base. Today, the men and women of the U.S. Air Force's 53rd Weather Reconnaissance Squadron continue to perform this dangerous job.

A couple is rescued from the roof of their house after the streets of New Orleans flooded from Hurricane Katrina.

Hurricane Isaac partially tested the new system in August 2012. It made landfall in southeastern Louisiana, east of the city. The new defenses protected much of the New Orleans area from an almost 11-foot (3-m) storm surge.

LONG-TERM FORECASTS

In addition to forecasting the strength and motion of particular storms, meteorologists can model or predict the total number of storms expected during a given season. The models take into account climate, ocean conditions, and world rainfall levels. The models also monitor wind and atmospheric pressure over the oceans where tropical cyclones form. The forecasts are revised over the course of the year. The models have become increasingly accurate at predicting the total number of storms during a season.

HOW SCIENCE WORKS
COMPUTER FORECAST MODELS

Meteorologists are able to make predictions about hurricane paths because they have measured and observed many hurricanes in the past. They make scientific assumptions that new hurricanes will react to conditions the same as past hurricanes. Meteorologists now better understand the patterns of hurricanes by measuring many of them with aircraft and satellites.

Meteorologists take the information on new storms and feed it into a computer forecast model. A computer forecast model is a set of equations that predicts where a storm will travel and how large it will become. The best models require computers with a high processing power, as well as a large amount of data about the storm. Computer modeling of tropical cyclone paths is better than it has ever been, but it still is not perfect. Models cannot always account for sudden changes in speed and direction. They also are not very accurate past 24 hours.

FOUR

ONE STORM, MANY DANGERS

Hurricane winds can rip an area apart in a matter of hours. Wind from a Category 3 hurricane is strong enough to blow out windows and rip off pieces of buildings. These objects become deadly flying debris. In the strongest storms, winds can reach 150 miles (240 km) per hour for long periods. Short gusts can be as fast as 200 miles (320 km) per hour. At these speeds, winds can carry debris straight through tree trunks. The storm winds can also topple trees and break power lines. A tree can fall on a person, crush a car, or break through a roof. A downed power line can electrocute anyone who accidentally touches or steps on it.

Hurricane winds can easily lift houses and cars.

Water from a storm surge floods buildings and turns streets into rivers.

COASTAL AREAS

Hurricanes bring an even bigger danger to coastal areas from the sea. When a hurricane moves toward land, its winds push a huge amount of seawater in front of the storm. This rise in sea level is called a storm surge and can span hundreds of miles. When it comes ashore, the storm surge can travel many miles inland. Rushing water can pick up and carry cars, tear down buildings, and drown people with powerful currents. Drowning was the most common cause of death from Superstorm Sandy, and most people died in flooded homes. Heavy objects in the water move through it at dangerous speeds. Cars, trees, street signs, telephone poles, and even boats can crash into buildings or people. Anything that breaks and floats away becomes part of this deadly mass. Seawater also destroys underground electrical equipment. Thousands or even millions of people might be without power for days or weeks at a time.

In some places, flash floods add to the danger. As a storm comes ashore and weakens, it releases its moisture as heavy rain. Often, a few feet of rain falls in a short period of time. Rivers and lakes can overflow

TYPHOON HAIYAN

Typhoon Haiyan was a tropical cyclone that devastated North Pacific countries including Palau, the Philippines, Vietnam, and China in November 2013. The typhoon killed thousands in the hardest-hit Philippines. Sustained winds, or winds that kept a relatively constant speed, were measured at 195 miles (314 km) per hour. The violent winds and a 20-foot (6-m) storm surge sent boats flying inland, reduced buildings to rubble, and caused people to drown. The official Filipino death toll of approximately 8,000 was not known until months after the catastrophe.

A storm surge hits the New England coast in 1938.

their banks, flooding neighborhoods. People can become trapped in flooded homes.

HIT AT HIGH TIDE

The Great New England Hurricane of 1938 devastated the coasts of New York, Connecticut, Rhode Island, Massachusetts, and other areas of the Northeast. Its storm surge flooded the coast during a very high tide. The result was catastrophic. Rhode Island experienced a storm surge of 17 feet (5 m) above the normal tide level. Massachusetts recorded tides of 18 to 25 feet (5.5 to 8 m). Approximately 600 people were killed. Property damage totaled more than $600 million.

HOW SCIENCE WORKS

Meteorologists have discovered that storm surges are even more dangerous if a hurricane hits at high tide. The tide is the constant change in sea level on shorelines, caused by the gravitational pull of the moon and sun on ocean water. High tide is the time of day when the water reaches its highest point.

A storm tide is the combination of the storm surge and the normal tide level. A 15-foot (4.5-m) storm surge combined with a 5-foot (1.5-m) tide will produce a 20-foot (6-m) storm tide. Because a storm surge can affect hundreds of miles of coastline, the combination of the surge and the tide can cause major destruction.

Meteorologists use many tools to measure tides and surges. Tide stations are permanent structures where calm tides can be measured. High watermarks on trees and structures near the coast show how high tides and surges have risen in the past. Pressure sensors are placed on structures in the path of a hurricane as the storm approaches. The sensors help meteorologists determine when water levels reach particular depths.

FIVE

MINIMIZING DAMAGE

In 2004, Hurricanes Alex, Charley, Frances, Gaston, Ivan, and Jeanne made landfall in the United States. These storms killed more than 3,000 people and caused more than $42.5 billion in damage. Hurricane Katrina hit in 2005, along with Hurricanes Cindy, Dennis, Rita, and Wilma. The combined damage from these storms topped $110 billion, and thousands of lives were lost. Superstorm Sandy caused $65 billion in damage on its own. These three hurricane seasons have shown the importance of protecting coastlines as a way to minimize damage.

Hurricane season can cost cities billions of dollars in damage.

The failure of the Industrial Canal levee in New Orleans led to flooding during Hurricane Rita.

SOFT AND HARD PROTECTION

Governments, meteorologists, and engineers look at soft and hard protections. Soft protections are natural. People

make hard protections, such as storm surge barriers, levees, and floodwalls that separate coastal areas from the sea. Storm surge barriers and floodwalls are built with concrete and steel. Some of these structures are more than 20 feet (6 m) high. The structures include moving gates and walls. The gates remain open during good weather and closed during a hurricane.

Levees can occur naturally or be made by people. These raised ridges are usually made of packed earth and held together with vegetation. Manufactured barriers offer protection, but building and maintaining them costs millions of dollars. Structures can also damage wetlands, swamps, and barrier islands that are often part of a coastal community.

Soft protection is nature's way of protecting an area from flooding, including tangles of trees, grasses, and other types of vegetation. These obstacles help to slow a surge. Maintaining and restoring these natural barriers can provide added protection.

INCREASED AMOUNTS OF SALT

Hurricanes carry huge amounts of seawater with them when they make landfall. In some cases, the seawater contains high levels of salt that are too much for affected plant and animal populations to bear. Habitats cannot get rid of the saltwater fast enough or do not have enough freshwater to replace it with. Plants and animals die if they cannot adapt to the salt.

Scientists at the National Hurricane Center in Florida help warn people about coming hurricanes.

CHANGING SEA LEVELS

The director of the National Weather Service, Louis Uccellini, spoke about higher sea levels after Typhoon Haiyan struck the Philippines in November 2013: "The fact that the sea levels are rising means that as you get these types of storm systems, you will be driving more water towards land."

CLOUD SEEDING

One radical idea for reducing the impact of tropical storms is cloud seeding, a form of geoengineering. Geoengineering is the process of trying to control Earth's weather or climate for human benefit. Cloud seeding is the act of adding chemicals to clouds to cause precipitation to fall. Aircraft, rockets, and cannons add chemicals to the clouds, and these chemicals cause raindrops to form around them. Then the raindrops fall earlier than they naturally would have. This helps scientists trying to control when and where rain will fall.

Still, these sea level changes will not necessarily make hurricanes more frequent in the near future. No hurricanes hit the United States in 2013. Meanwhile, meteorologists and governments continue working to find better ways of protecting lives, land, and property. Better warning systems will help people prepare for hurricanes. Stronger barriers help minimize dangerous storm surges, but these solutions will not remove all risks. However, they do provide people with more time to prepare for, avoid, and survive these deadly storms.

CASE STUDY

IMPROVING DEFENSES AFTER KATRINA

Hurricane Katrina devastated New Orleans. More than 10 inches (25 cm) of rain fell in 24 hours. In some places, water reached more than 20 feet (6 m) high.

Much of the flooding happened because the flood protection systems failed. The water rose above or broke through more than 50 levees. Pumping the water out also became difficult because many pumping stations, which are used to regulate rainfall and drainage in the bowl-shaped city, were not working.

The U.S. Army Corps of Engineers (USACE) is responsible for building and maintaining New Orleans' flood defenses. After Hurricane Katrina, the organization found many outdated, weakened, and unfinished defenses.

The USACE has been building a new system and strengthening other portions. The new system includes higher and better-constructed levees, as well as floodwalls and storm surge barriers.

TOP TEN WORST HURRICANES

1. BHOLA CYCLONE, 1970

This was perhaps the deadliest tropical storm ever recorded. Between 300,000 and 500,000 people were killed in Bangladesh, mostly as a result of drowning due to a massive storm surge.

2. CYCLONE NARGIS, 2008

This cyclone tore through Myanmar and exposed the country's poor infrastructure and the inability to deliver aid to its people. The storm's death toll is estimated at 138,000.

3. THE GREAT HURRICANE OF 1780

This monster storm killed approximately 22,000 people when it blasted Barbados, Martinique, St. Lucia, and other Caribbean islands.

4. HURRICANE MITCH, 1998

Slow-moving Hurricane Mitch devastated Honduras, Guatemala, and Nicaragua with its ferocious winds, heavy rainstorms, deadly mudslides, and severe flooding. More than 11,000 people died.

5. GALVESTON HURRICANE, 1900

With up to a 15-foot (5-m) storm surge and flash flooding, this hurricane drowned the city of Galveston, Texas. It took more than 6,000 lives, making it the deadliest hurricane ever to hit the United States.

6. TYPHOON HAIYAN, 2013

Typhoon Haiyan damaged the Philippines and other Pacific nations in 2013. It killed more than 6,000 people.

7. OKEECHOBEE HURRICANE, 1928

This tropical cyclone was the second deadliest in U.S. history. It formed off the west coast of Africa and was a Category 4 storm by the time it made landfall in southern Florida. Approximately 2,500 people were killed.

8. CHENIÈRE CAMINADA HURRICANE, 1893

This hurricane destroyed the fishing village of Caminadaville, Louisiana, and killed more than 2,000 people.

9. HURRICANE KATRINA, 2005

Hurricane Katrina devastated New Orleans and other areas of the Gulf Coast. In New Orleans, floodwater covered more than 80 percent of the city. The hurricane killed more than 1,800 people.

10. FLORIDA KEYS LABOR DAY HURRICANE, 1935

This Category 5 storm is considered the strongest to hit the United States in the 1900s. It killed approximately 400 people.

GLOSSARY

ANEMOMETERS: Instruments used to measure wind speed.

BAROMETERS: Instruments that measure air pressure in the atmosphere.

CONDENSES: Turns from a gas into a liquid.

ENGINEERS: People who design and build things that solve problems.

EVACUATION: A movement of people out of a particular area.

EYE: A cloud-free area of light winds in the center of a hurricane.

EYEWALL: A violent wall of tall thunderstorms surrounding the eye and containing the heaviest rain and the strongest winds of the storm.

HUMID: A lot of moisture in the air.

RAIN GAUGES: Instruments used to measure an amount of rainfall.

RAINBANDS: Long bands of rain clouds that spiral outward from the eyewall.

SATELLITES: Objects that move in a curved path around a planet.

STORM SURGE: A huge rise in seawater produced by a hurricane's winds.

TELEGRAPH: An early device used to send electronic signals through wires.

FURTHER INFORMATION

BOOKS

Jeffrey, Gary. *Hurricane Hunters & Tornado Chasers*. New York: Rosen, 2008.

Silverstein, Alvin. *Hurricanes: The Science Behind Killer Storms*. Berkeley Heights, NJ: Enslow, 2009.

Simon, Seymour. *Hurricanes*. New York: HarperCollins, 2007.

WEBSITES

http://video.nationalgeographic.com/video/kids/forces-of-nature-kids/hurricanes-101-kids
This website has a video that shows the destructive power of hurricanes. Three-dimensional computer graphics show how hurricanes form and cause damage.

http://www.ready.gov/kids/know-the-facts/hurricanes
This website features important information you can use to stay safe during a hurricane.

INDEX